Life musings…

Korina Gosling-Cowdery

BookLeaf Publishing

India | USA | UK

Presentation by *BookLeaf Publishing*

Web: www.bookleafpub.com

E-mail: info@bookleafpub.com

ISBN: 9789358737158

First edition 2023

Denial

I miss the way you made me laugh
and how we shouted and cried
I miss the way we made it up
but mostly I miss you by my side

You used to tell me everything's alright
We've faced so many tests together
Our love always had the strength to fight
I'm sorry this one got the better

I miss the feel of you on my skin
the warmth of your arms around me
the kiss of your lips upon my mouth
and how we fitted together perfectly

Out of all the things I could possibly have
none compare to you
Because all the plans and dreams we had
together
Would have been amazing, if only they came
true

Letting go…

I'm the one that you notice the least,
yet you are always in my thoughts,
I try to convince myself the feelings have
ceased,
that the battle between us has been fought.

Still every time I see your face, I know deep
inside,
that I wish to be with you on your journey in
life,
that everything you accomplish, you have my
pride
And that I'd never want to cause you any strife

You've gone your way and I've gone mine
but I hope you know I'm with you to the end.
I'll be the one with you, no concept of time
in the wait and hope that you'll call me a friend.

Indecision

Talk to those that are younger to justify your
decision
Talk to those of the same age to make your
decision
Talk to those that are older to make the right
decision
Feel at ease with how to proceed

Regression

I've got a bee in my bonnet,
A myth that needs to be dispelled:
That going to work is harder than
keeping a tiny human alive

To keep them fed, clean and entertained-
but not too much, of course!
To be well rested and in order to do this,
You need to look after yourself...

But you have a tiny dictator
on when you can eat and go to the loo,
And a lack of hot drinks
to see you through

My body is aching from the manual lifting
Where are the adults? My spirit is sinking,
Let's all agree that both are tough
And do those nightly wakings together-
Because they're so bloody rough!

Change

Power is a fickle thing
When you have it, boy does it sting
Yet it sparks the embers deep inside
Enjoy it now for I'll come back in time

If it puts a fire in your belly
And an ache in your heart
There's no doubt about it
That's the best time to start

Sister

A friend from the start,
And always there in your heart.
No matter the path of life: smile or tear,
A constant comfort to see or hear.

Sometimes

You can't fit anymore friends into your life,
others you are on look out for new ones more
suited to who you currently are;
sometimes you're desperate to find that
friendship that clicks.
It changes-keep riding the waves,
some days at sea are better than others.
Find all weather friends not fine weather friends.

To those passed

I can see you in my thoughts-
That is a special thing,
for all the money in the world.
Those that overpower will not win.

Your words and phrases come to life
as does the sun in spring.
This kind and gentle family...
what secrets can it bring?

To always think of others
and know what makes them sing
can only mean where you are now
is infinitely better than living...

Tuesday

On the eve of the anniversary of
the day you were born,
what is there to ponder?
What is there to mourn?
Search for the highlights in the grey of memory,
and know there are openings beyond yet we can
see.
So when this day around the sun returns-
You'll hopefully know: you are loved, you are
needed more than you are shown.

Celebration

We've had a bit of a talk,
this will really make you squawk.
So do let us know,
when you would like to go,
because we're ready to pop the cork!

Friendship

There's nothing quite as special,
as a friendship tried and true;
that feeling of encouragement,
in everything you do.
And when that friendship,
never fails to give your heart a lift,
it's then you know,
that you have found,
a very special gift!

Looking back…

Why are you standing at the door?
Why don't you crawl anymore?
First year=danger of failure to thrive
Second year=danger of failure to survive
Third year=danger of failure to stay alive.

Loneliness

The silence that makes your mind echo,
Who is reaching out for me?
The recognition of feeling low.
Reaching out is the key.
Keep on getting through the days,
It's true that better ones are on the way.

Heartbreak

When things change,
and you're not ready...
Follow this advice,
to keep you steady.

Acknowledge and process how you feel,
let others see it so support is real.
Time is the only constant healer,
calm and growth will return to her.

Thank you

You met me when I was in need,
you always know what to do.
You met me when times were hard,
and when they were good too.

I met you with love in my heart,
an endless want to see you smile.
I met you to go on adventures,
learning life's lessons all the while.

Today I meet you all here together,
the support and love to receive.
Today I meet you with a thank you,
for the joy you've helped us weave.

You've embraced the decisions I've made,
including when I became a we,
and I couldn't end without thanking my love,
for meeting and choosing me.

Strike

Lazy. We all have to
pay. Pay?
Strike.
Brave. We all have to
support education,
support children,
support parents.
If we have one choice
towards a voice-
this is it...

Grateful

Five years, festive time, time for reflection.
As my baby makes her presence known,
the gentle rolls-the solid presses
My own little blessing!

A house built for us-with its now decorated
rooms;
Our eldest asleep in her bed,
what joy of Christmas morn lies ahead?

Travel and study have both taken place
and so too has family time-relationships shift.
Jobs have come and gone
and this must not be missed...

Time has shown yet again that
Anything can be fixed!

Versions

I'm not the same person that walked through the
door,
And yet I recognise that I've seen her before.
New start, fresh outlook, ready to meet people
who
could only be described as the allies to get you
through.
It is them that I miss when the holidays run
round
And I'm sinking deeper underground,
Waiting for when I'm allowed to call
And finally return to the building of school.
No longer do I want or need to feel like this,
Walk through the door into untimely bliss 🖤

www.ingramcontent.com/pod-product-compliance
Lightning Source LLC
LaVergne TN
LVHW050313200726
843509LV00015B/3293